A Hutterite Colouring Book
Ein Hutterisches Malbuch
LaDonna Stahl

August 2018

© **2018 Ladonna Stahl.** All rights reserved.
The work herein may not be photocopied or otherwise
replicated without permission from the publisher.

ISBN 978-1-927913-82-6

First printing, October 2018
Second printing, December 2018

Box 40 • MacGregor, MB • R0H 0R0
p. 204–272–5132 • f. 204–252–2381 • e. orders@hbbookcentre.com

Printed in Canada.

www.ingramcontent.com/pod-product-compliance
Lightning Source LLC
Chambersburg PA
CBHW051355110526
44592CB00024B/2993